XTREME INSECTS

Ants

BY S.L. HAMILTON

A&D Xtreme
An imprint of Abdo Publishing | www.abdopublishing.com

Visit us at
www.abdopublishing.com

Printed in the United States of America, North Mankato, Minnesota.
102014
012015

 PRINTED ON RECYCLED PAPER

Editor: John Hamilton
Graphic Design: John Hamilton
Cover Design: Sue Hamilton
Cover Photo: Corbis
Interior Photos: Alamy, p. 17; iStock Images, pp. 1, 2-3, 4-5, 6-7, 14, 15, 30-31; John Hamilton, p.32; Minden Pictures, pp. 10-11, 12-13, 16, 20-21, 22, 22-23, 24, 28; Science Source Images, pp. 8, 9, 11, 18-19, 25, 26, 27, 29.

Websites
To learn more about Xtreme Insects, visit booklinks.abdopublishing.com. These links are routinely monitored and updated to provide the most current information available.

Library of Congress Control Number: 2014944880

Cataloging-in-Publication Data

Hamilton, S.L.
 Ants / S.L. Hamilton.
  p. cm. -- (Xtreme insects)
 ISBN 978-1-62403-686-6 (lib. bdg.)
 Includes index.
 1. Ants--Juvenile literature.   I. Title.
 595.79/6--dc23

2014944880

Contents

Ants

Ants are tiny powerhouses that live in groups called colonies, which are led by queens. Colonies range in size from a few dozen ants to many millions. Scientists have identified more than 12,000 species of ants. They vary in size, color, and behavior. Some are fierce biters. Some are great builders. Some are destructive, while others help rid places of pests.

Ants work together, growing their colonies through hard work, amazing abilities, and sometimes extreme defenses.

XTREME FACT – There are trillions of ants worldwide. Only extremely cold places such as Iceland, Greenland, and Antarctica, do not have ants.

Body Parts

Like all insects, ants have three body parts: head, thorax, and abdomen. The thorax, or middle region, of an ant's body holds all six of its jointed legs.

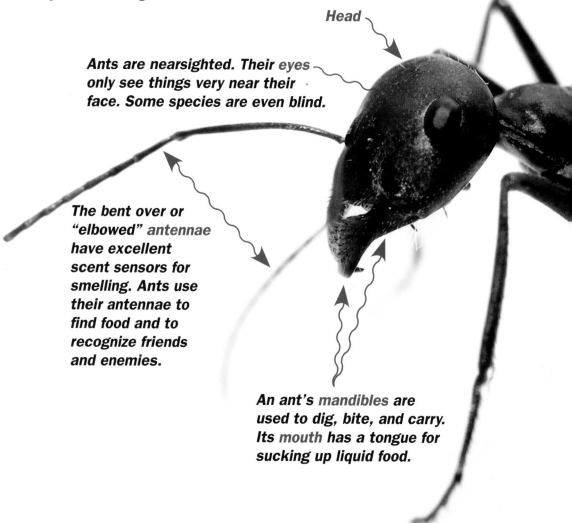

Head

Ants are nearsighted. Their eyes only see things very near their face. Some species are even blind.

The bent over or "elbowed" antennae have excellent scent sensors for smelling. Ants use their antennae to find food and to recognize friends and enemies.

An ant's mandibles are used to dig, bite, and carry. Its mouth has a tongue for sucking up liquid food.

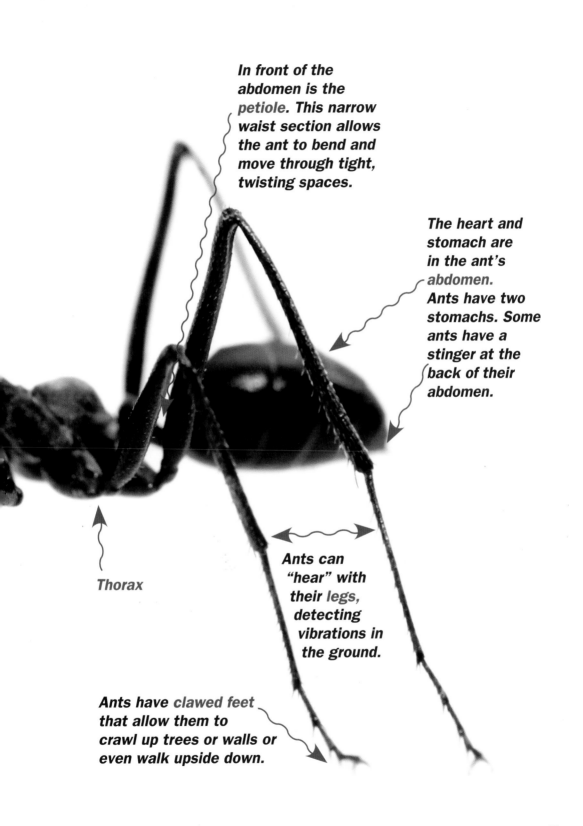

In front of the abdomen is the *petiole*. This narrow waist section allows the ant to bend and move through tight, twisting spaces.

The heart and stomach are in the ant's *abdomen*. Ants have two stomachs. Some ants have a stinger at the back of their abdomen.

Thorax

Ants can "hear" with their *legs*, detecting vibrations in the ground.

Ants have *clawed feet* that allow them to crawl up trees or walls or even walk upside down.

Bullet Ants

Ants may be small, but some species are armed with stingers. The most powerful ant venom comes from the bullet ant. One-inch (2.5-cm) -long bullet ants are found in the forests of Central and South America. People who have been stung by bullet ants say it is like being shot. The bullet ant is also called the "24 ant." Once stung, a person will feel the intense pain for 24 hours.

The Schmidt Sting Pain Index rates the bullet ant sting as the number-one most painful of all insects. Bullet ants latch onto the skin with their mandibles, then inject venom with their abdomen's stinger.

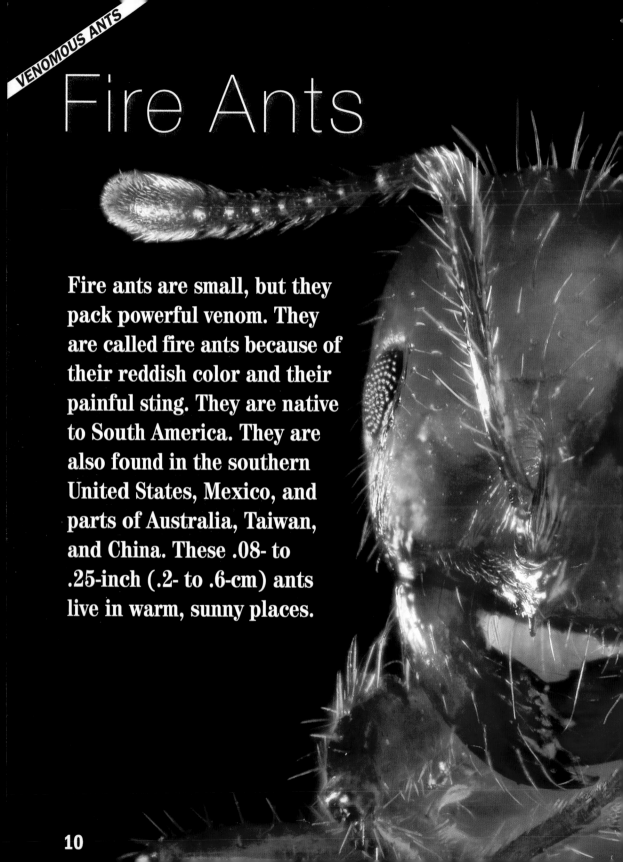

Fire Ants

Fire ants are small, but they pack powerful venom. They are called fire ants because of their reddish color and their painful sting. They are native to South America. They are also found in the southern United States, Mexico, and parts of Australia, Taiwan, and China. These .08- to .25-inch (.2- to .6-cm) ants live in warm, sunny places.

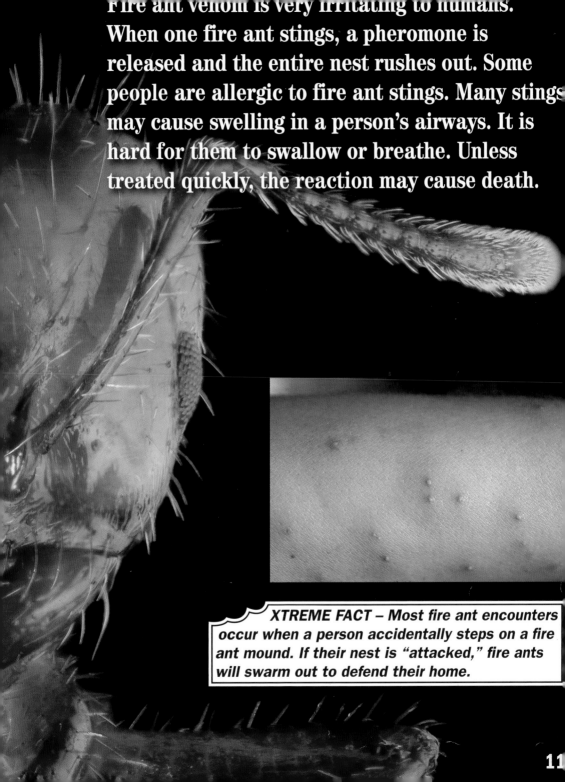

Fire ant venom is very irritating to humans. When one fire ant stings, a pheromone is released and the entire nest rushes out. Some people are allergic to fire ant stings. Many stings may cause swelling in a person's airways. It is hard for them to swallow or breathe. Unless treated quickly, the reaction may cause death.

XTREME FACT – Most fire ant encounters occur when a person accidentally steps on a fire ant mound. If their nest is "attacked," fire ants will swarm out to defend their home.

Harvester Ants

Maricopa harvester ants are .25 to .4 inch (.6 to 1 cm) long. They are armed with the most toxic venom known in the insect world. In addition, this native of the American Southwest delivers a vicious bite using its powerful mandibles. Like their fire ant cousins, harvester ants latch onto their prey's skin, then move in a circle, injecting a ring of savage stings. Some attacks cause dangerous allergic reactions in humans. The pain from a bite lasts about four hours.

XTREME FACT– *Twelve stings from a Maricopa harvester ant is enough to kill a 4.4-pound (2-kg) rat.*

A large Maricopa harvester ant invading a nest of smaller ants.

Carpenter Ants

Some ants are known for their vicious bites. Carpenter ants may grow to .5 inch (1.3 cm) in length. They have big mandibles. If disturbed, they can bite their prey and spray formic acid into the open wound. These North American ants live near damp, rotting, or hollow wood.

Leafcutter Ants

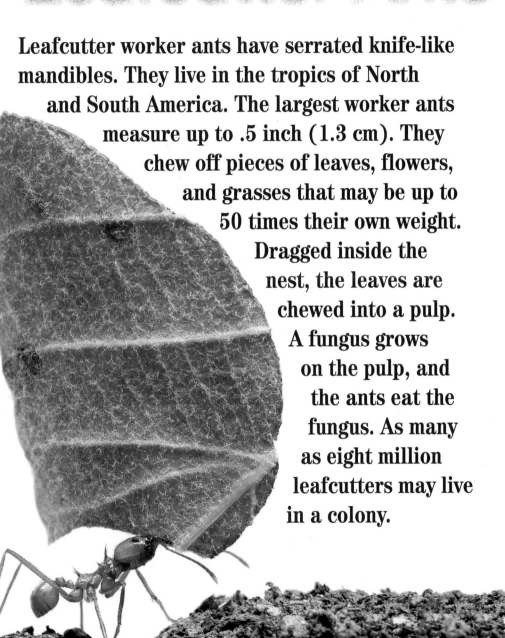

Leafcutter worker ants have serrated knife-like mandibles. They live in the tropics of North and South America. The largest worker ants measure up to .5 inch (1.3 cm). They chew off pieces of leaves, flowers, and grasses that may be up to 50 times their own weight. Dragged inside the nest, the leaves are chewed into a pulp. A fungus grows on the pulp, and the ants eat the fungus. As many as eight million leafcutters may live in a colony.

Jumping Jack Ants

Jumping jack ants, also known as jack jumper ants, are found in Australia. They hop when they are upset. A type of bull ant, they measure .3 inch (.8 cm). They attack their prey with powerful mandibles and venomous stingers. Unlike most ants, they have excellent eyesight.

Trap-Jaw Ants

Trap-jaw ants are found in North, Central, and South America. They have the fastest-closing jaws of any creature. Sensitive hairs line the mandibles. When the hairs are touched, the jaws snap shut at speeds up to 145 miles per hour (233 kph). Trap-jaw ants can also escape from prey by hopping up to 3.3 inches (8.4 cm) into the air.

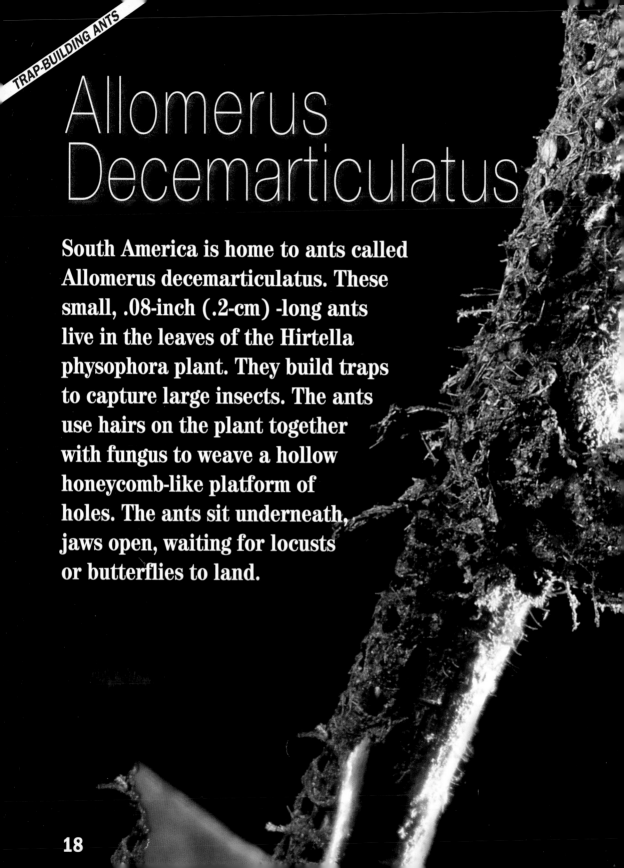

Allomerus Decemarticulatus

South America is home to ants called Allomerus decemarticulatus. These small, .08-inch (.2-cm) -long ants live in the leaves of the Hirtella physophora plant. They build traps to capture large insects. The ants use hairs on the plant together with fungus to weave a hollow honeycomb-like platform of holes. The ants sit underneath, jaws open, waiting for locusts or butterflies to land.

The ants grab onto their prey's arms, legs, and antenna and pull. Other ants from the colony move in to sting and bite. The ants then bring the prey back to their home in the leaves and divide it into a tasty meal for the colony.

XTREME FACT– The Hirtella physophora plant also benefits from the Allomerus ants. The ants protect the plant from insects and parasites that would kill it.

Argentine Ants

Argentine ants are only .1 inch (.3 cm) long, but they create large colonies and nests. Native to South America, Argentine ants have spread around the world. The largest colony is in Europe. It sprawls from Italy to Portugal, covering 3,728 miles (6,000 km). There may be as many as one billion ants in this super colony. These massive colonies are known to kill off other ant species, as well as wildlife unfortunate enough to be swarmed. Argentine ants are not poisonous, but they have a fierce bite.

Argentine ants eating a dead piranha fish on a riverbank in northern Argentina.

Army Ants

Army ants are found in tropical forests and jungles in Central and South America and Africa. They march as an army of between 150,000 to 2 million ants. They interlock their legs and use their own bodies to build bridges over water or create ceilings and walls to protect their queen from bad weather and predators. They stop long enough for the queen to lay eggs, which allows for a new generation to hatch. Then, they are on the move again.

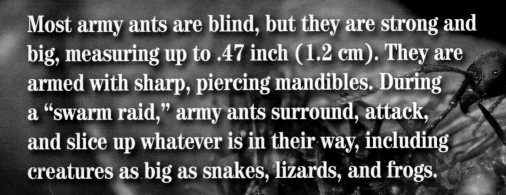

Most army ants are blind, but they are strong and big, measuring up to .47 inch (1.2 cm). They are armed with sharp, piercing mandibles. During a "swarm raid," army ants surround, attack, and slice up whatever is in their way, including creatures as big as snakes, lizards, and frogs.

XTREME FACT – People can hear the sound of thousands of army ants marching across the ground. If ants travel through a person's house, the one advantage is that they eat all insect pests that do not get out of their way.

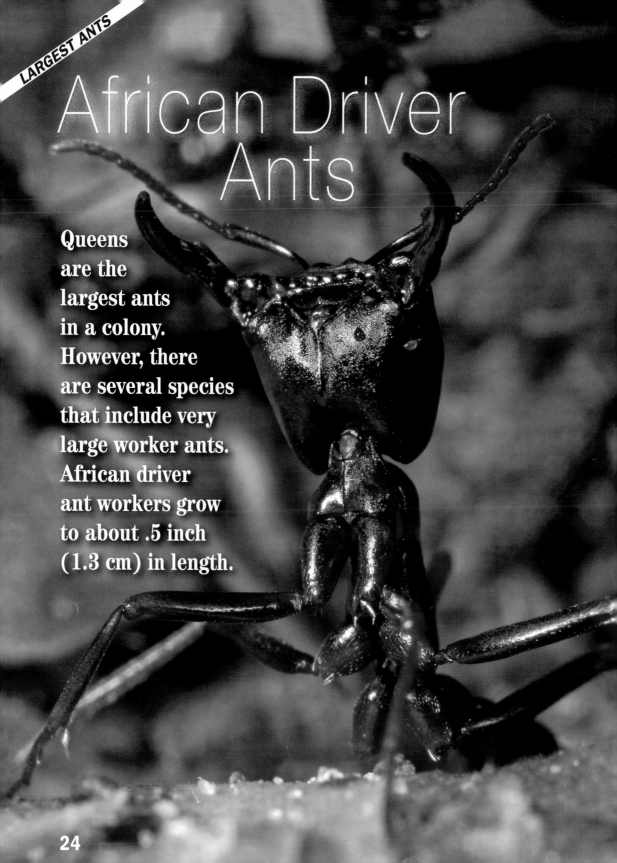

African Driver Ants

Queens are the largest ants in a colony. However, there are several species that include very large worker ants. African driver ant workers grow to about .5 inch (1.3 cm) in length.

Dinoponera

Dinoponera gigantea ants are found in the tropical forests of South America. They may grow up to 1.2 inches (3 cm) in length, making them one of the largest ant species on Earth. They prefer to nest in shallow burrows at the base of trees.

Ants Used in Medicine

Leafcutter ants have bacteria on their bodies that keep their fungus gardens from being overrun by parasites. The bacteria are similar to those used by humans to make antibiotics. Scientists are researching it, hoping to make potentially lifesaving medicine.

To close a wound in an emergency, some people allow leafcutter or army ants to bite them, then pull off the body. The head and mandibles remain, holding the skin closed like a suture (stitch).

Can You
Eat Them?

About 313 species of ants are edible. In China, there are black ant farms. Some people eat them deep fried. They believe it eases arthritis pain. Wood ant eggs taste like shrimp. North American carpenter ants smell bad, but are edible. Eating honeypot ants is like eating candy, while leafcutter ants have a bacon-pistachio taste. They are sold as treats in movie theaters in Columbia.

Honeypot ants

A man eating large toasted ants.

XTREME FACT – There are about one million ants to each human. The weight of all ants roughly matches the weight of all humans on Earth.

Glossary

ANTENNAE
Long, thin appendages on an insect's head that act as sensors for such things as vibrations or scents. Ants use their antennae to find food, and to distinguish between friendly ants and those of enemy colonies.

BACTERIA
Single-celled organisms that often cause illness and disease in humans.

BURROW
An underground home.

COLONY
A group of creatures, such as ants, that live closely together. Depending on the species, ants live in colonies that number between several hundred to two or three million or more.

MANDIBLES
Strong, beak-like mouth organs that are used for grabbing and biting.

PHEROMONE
A scented chemical substance given off by some insects that tells them how to behave.

Queen

Ant colonies are divided into three main groups: queens, males, and workers (which include soldiers that defend the colony). The queen is the largest ant in the colony. Her main job is to lay eggs, which hatch into new generations of ants that repopulate the colony. Queens can lay thousands of eggs in their lifetime. Some colonies include several queens, while others have just one.

Schmidt Sting Pain Index

A scale that rates the painfulness of stings, ranging from 0 (least painful) to 4 (most painful). It was invented by Justin Schmidt, an American entomologist (insect scientist). Common bee stings are rated 2. The bullet ant has a pain index of 4. It is described as producing "immediate, excruciating pain and numbness to pencil-point pressure, as well as trembling in the form of a totally uncontrollable urge to shake the affected part."

Species

A group of living things that have similar looks and behaviors, but are not identical. They are often called by a similar name. For example, scientists have classified more than 12,000 species of ants.

Thorax

The middle section of an insect's body between the head and the abdomen.

Index